COUSIN JOHN

COUSIN JOHN

The Story of a Boy and a Small Smart Pig

WALTER PAINE
illustrated by Bert Dodson

BUNKER HILL PUBLISHING

First published in 2006
by Bunker Hill Publishing Inc.
285 River Road, Piermont
New Hampshire 03779, USA

10 9 8 7 6 5 4 3 2 1

Library of Congress Cataloguing in Publication Data
is available from the publisher's office

ISBN 1 59373 057 8

Designed by Louise Millar

Printed in China by Jade Productions Ltd

For my grandchildren

Foreword
A passionate curiosity

I've known Walter since 1978, when I began work at the Montshire Museum. But not until I asked him to help me with an exhibit of beetles several years later did I really begin to *know* him. Out from under his carapace emerged a most remarkable person – a warm, humorous, articulate man in the tradition of the great nineteenth-century naturalists, those amateurs (read "lovers") who contributed so much to our understanding of other creatures.

An accomplished student of his specialties, beetles and mollusks, Walter is also deeply committed to bringing science to life for others. He laughingly tells of his entanglement with the Montshire Museum in its earliest days. It happened when he was editor/publisher of our regional daily newspaper and a pillar of the community. As the director of the fledgling museum was passing by the newspaper plant on his lunch hour, he spotted Walter leaping through a neighboring field, swishing an insect net across the goldenrod. *That's my man*, he thought, and that day Walter himself became the "catch."

Aldo Leopold says in *A Sand County Almanac*. "There are some who can live without wild things, and some who cannot." Clearly, Walter is one of those lucky people who cannot. Beneath this tale of a boy's difficult and yearning relationship with his father, and the less complex pleasures of life with a pet pig, is another story: the sustaining power of a passionate curiosity about the natural world.

JOAN WALTERMIRE, CURATOR OF EXHIBITS,
MONTSHIRE MUSEUM OF SCIENCE
NORWICH, VERMONT

"There is always one moment in childhood
when the door opens and lets the future in."

– GRAHAM GREENE

Contents

CHAPTER ONE

A Magic Kingdom

I grew up in a funny old brick house on a steep hillside in Brookline, Massachusetts, just far enough outside Boston to be considered the "country" back in 1932. From a distance you would have thought it was the largest house you'd ever seen. But it wasn't the mansion it appeared to be, because, if you saw our three-story house end-on, you would realize that it was only one room wide!

A long, skinny corridor connected the rooms on the second floor where we children slept with our parents' quarters at the opposite end. I was 9 years old, and on rainy days there was nothing quite like racing up and down that hallway, narrowly avoiding collisions with other members of the household.

On good days, though, I preferred the outdoors and loved to roam the open acres around us. There, among the fragrant fields and massive maples, oaks, hickories, elms, and beech, I found so many creatures, both real and imaginary, that I called it "My Magic Kingdom."

At the bottom of the hill was an old farm, with a big barn, silo, tool shed, and henhouse, all painted dark green. In the fenced area between them, we kept rabbits, occasional lambs, and a grouchy goat I called Greenhorn because of the paint on his horns from constantly butting the fence.

I disliked Greenhorn. He was bigger and stronger than I was; his horns were sharp and so was his smell. I did my best to avoid him while I cared for my rabbit, Whiskers, and helped Dad collect the eggs laid by our flock of Rhode Island Reds. Every spring we raised hens from chicks hatched in an incubator in Dad's study. It was my job to turn the eggs now and then, just as a mother hen does on her nest, and to listen for the first faint "peck-peck" that told us chicks were about to hatch.

When my father was with me, I pretended to be unafraid of Greenhorn. When he wasn't, I brought along carrot tops, beet greens, and old lettuce leaves to occupy the goat while I fed Whiskers, who shared the same enclosure. Even so, if I was slow to close the gate on leaving, I could expect a good thump on my behind, a sign, I suppose, of Greenhorn's appreciation.

I longed for a companion to share my ramblings on the hill, but Whiskers wasn't much of a playmate. Often, when I picked him up, he stomped my chest or peed on my shirt – or both. Brothers or sisters could be wonderful playmates, except that mine were still too young to join in my adventures.

From time to time, Mother suggested that I find a buddy among the numerous cousins who lived nearby. That never seemed to work because the only cousins I got along with didn't share my excitement about nature. I needed a different kind of friend, and not necessarily a human one. If an animal, I knew it would have to be more of a pal than a pet. I dismissed dogs because most of them liked to chase wild things.

My friend Harry kept a pet boa constrictor in a heated cage. He would sit and watch it eat white rats his dad brought home from a laboratory. The rest of the time it slept. I thought that was all pretty boring. Besides, I couldn't see how truly wild creatures could be content away from their natural homes. Do you think the wild animals you've seen in the zoo look happy? I don't.

I therefore felt fortunate to live in the country where I could hear the cock pheasant's call, telling me it was time to be up and about. I liked to slip out, barefoot in the dewy grass, to a special place between the knobby roots of a big beech at the meadow's edge where, if I was lucky, I could watch a red fox leaping high to flush a vole, or a hen pheasant foraging watchfully with her chicks.

*"A special place...where I could watch
a red fox leaping high to flush a vole."*

One day, I saw a fox about to nab a critter when, with a sudden *whoosh* overhead, a small hawk snatched it from under the animal's nose. The puzzled fox sat quietly on its haunches, head cocked to one side, as if trying to figure what had happened to breakfast.

Morning excursions were never the same; there was always something new to see, hear, smell, catch, or just plain think about. I did a lot of that, and it was easy to lose track of time. "You have a watch," my father once said sternly, "so use it from now on, or you'll go hungry." Since breakfast was my favorite meal, I wasn't late again. But there was more than simply being on time – I craved my father's approval. The fact was that Dad and I had problems communicating. For one thing, he was a very reserved, hard-working business man, and I found it hard to talk to him because he always seemed preoccupied and showed little interest in what I was up to. I knew he went to his Boston office every work day, but I didn't know what he did there. After all, what does a 9 year old know about the world of business?

Mother wasn't much help. "He's in business with two partners, dear," she would explain, "but he doesn't like to discuss business at home." On weekends, if he wasn't entertaining friends, Dad was often totally absorbed with making reproduction English furniture in his workshop down the hill. I loved the sight and sound of the lathe's whirring leather belts and pulleys and the fragrance of the mahogany as it spun from the turning. But somehow I knew that Dad wasn't comfortable with me close by and watching him.

Aware of my frustration, Mother did her best to encourage me. "Be patient," she'd say, "Wait for the right moment to ask your questions." But problems persisted because the moments I chose never seemed to be the "right" ones. I had begun to feel sorry for myself, especially when kids at school described the great times they were having with their dads. It was then that my father surprised and delighted me by doing something totally unexpected. He built me a small workbench, complete with simple tools, in a corner of his shop.

Perhaps he figured that if I had my own projects, I would be less likely to disturb him. If so, it didn't work out that way. I wanted to please him by building things right, but since he was so involved with his furniture, he didn't show me how to use the tools he'd given me. So, I continued to pester him with questions.

Things came to a head one weekend when I distracted him just as he was feathering the edge of a delicate pie crust table top, causing his gouge to slip. "Damn!" he yelled, flinging the tool on the bench, "Now I've ruined it!" Then came a silent glare that plainly said, *If you know what's good for you, you better get out of here!* I did, and it was quite some time before I found courage to go back and finish my bird house.

I sought consolation for my difficulties with Dad among the creatures of our hill. I became a tireless observer, spying on the lives of skunks, squirrels, chipmunks, voles, woodchucks, rabbits, raccoons, foxes, pheasants, and the occasional owl or hawk. Some were predictable, and eventually I learned where to find them at various times of day. And I discovered something else: If I really wanted to learn more about these creatures, I must be very quiet (which was difficult) and stay very still (which was even more difficult), so they could get accustomed to my presence.

But no matter where I happened to be, I was expected home for tea at five o'clock. Sometimes I was late. Once, intrigued by the sudden appearance of a dark-eyed owl in my favorite climbing tree, I missed tea altogether. Dad didn't say anything, but his disapproving look told me what he thought. Still, as long as I stayed on the hill, I was free to explore and learn from my own mistakes. I recall one in particular while playing the bold hunter with my first BB gun. I dropped a gray squirrel from a lofty oak, and as it lay twitching pathetically at my feet, I felt a sudden surge of shame and sorrow for taking an innocent creature's life.

Gradually, I ventured deeper into the dark thickets crowning the hill. Poking around in the brush one day, I was startled to discover a circular mound of stones more than twice my height. Big boulders formed the base for layers of smaller ones neatly piled on top. Wedging my toes in the cracks, I worked my way up to where I could see that the center was also filled with rocks, the kind our local farmers were forever picking from their fields. It was a spooky place at first, but soon I got to like it, especially when I realized that when I stretched out on top, no one could see me from below.

I spent many happy hours atop this secret hideaway, luring resident squirrels with peanuts or imagining that I was an Indian scout, a pirate with his treasure or a patriot, keeping an eye on British Redcoats around Boston. I knew it was just a pile of old stones. But it was mine, because I found it, and if I didn't tell anyone else, only my animal friends would know where to find me.

CHAPTER TWO
A Light in the Window

S hortly before my tenth birthday, my parents decided I should trade my small room on the second floor for a larger one in the attic, in what was once the servants' quarters. I wasn't sure why. Maybe it was because I wandered into their bedroom at odd hours. More likely, it was because I had begun to collect all kinds of messy things: animal skins, bones, insects, and recently vacated turtle shells. I also produced some really stinky smells with my Porter Chemistry Set.

I liked being alone up there under the sloping eaves where rain pattered softly on the slates above my head, and winter brought sudden thunderous booms when snow slides struck the ground three floors below.

At night, as I lay in bed, I could hear mysterious scuffling, gnawing and chattering coming from behind small doors that led to crawl spaces under the eaves. But the best thing about my attic aerie was the empty room next door where I could begin to display my natural treasures.

In my *Young Naturalist's Handbook* I read that a light placed in front of a sheet in an open window would attract all sorts of critters. One warm spring evening, I tried it. The results were spectacular! Insects galore bombarded the sheet: noisy June bugs and big floppy moths, including a gorgeous Luna with pale green wings, a furry white body, feathery antennae and glowing red eyes. Then, suddenly, in swooped a bat in hot pursuit of a meal.

I'd never seen a bat up close. Just as I was trying to figure out how it could zip around the room so fast without hitting anything, it disappeared, but not out the window. In my excitement, I'd forgotten to close the door that led to the floors below! Too late! Already a column of insects and probably the bat as well, were streaming downward toward my parents' room. That meant *big* trouble!

First came a shriek from Mother. Then I heard Dad growl, "Walter must be up to something again – I better get the tennis racquet!" Down I raced with my butterfly net and together we managed to corner most of the intruders, except for the bat, which careened about just beyond our reach.

It was a funny scene, mother cowering under the covers while Dad danced around the bed in his blue and white striped nightshirt, wildly swinging at the bat, which vanished before he could catch it, most likely up a chimney.

"Dad danced around the bed...wildly swinging at the bat."

At breakfast next morning I tried to make conversation by explaining that June "bugs" were not really bugs at all, and why light was so attractive to moths. Whether bored or just plain exhausted, my parents weren't much interested in their evening visitors. What I got instead was a scolding for removing window screens at night. But that wasn't the end of my night collecting, because something else had happened: I learned that the night had its own creatures, which were just as intriguing as those seen by day. I continued to run my light trap, but from a window where my parents couldn't see it. Of course, I made sure to close my door!

Armed with Dad's magnifying glass and a notebook, I began to disturb the lives of bees and beetles, ants, moths, and butterflies, day and night. In the fall I roamed the hillside searching for cocoons. I kept them in a cool place until spring, so that I could watch the colorful creatures emerge and spread their wings.

One place I loved to visit was the Society for Natural History in Boston, with its displays of stuffed birds, mammals, reptiles, and insects. A huge whale skeleton hung from the high ceiling. I was there the day a big chunk of whalebone fell to the floor with a mighty crash, just missing a group of visitors. I kept hoping to be there if it happened again.

Dad's friends knew of my interest in nature, and they brought me creatures from far away places. They included a stuffed pair of Chinese golden pheasants, colorful Cuban land snails, and a big Amazonian turtle shell. On rainy days, I struggled, unsuccessfully, to make labels for my specimens that would look like the neat ones in the Society's collections.

Like their traveling friends, my parents also liked to take long trips abroad. The housekeeper who replaced them insisted I stay close, where she could keep an eye on me. I was allowed as far as the farm to do my daily chores, but it always seemed a long, lonely time, because apart from missing my parents, I really missed my animal friends on the hill.

This restriction on my ramblings was doubly frustrating because, at Mother's urging, I was just getting to know my Paine grandparents who lived above us on the hilltop. She seemed to be hinting that if I became friendly with my grandfather, I might get a better understanding of my own father's odd ways with me. This took some doing because I knew Grandpa only from occasional formal Sunday luncheons, mostly at his house. On these occasions, his tall, spare figure and sallow, finely drawn features reminded me of the Spanish grandee pictured in one of the books Dad had read aloud. To me, both were intimidating.

Although his parents lived so nearby, Dad seldom mentioned his father. But he spoke often of Grandma, a plump, pleasant woman, whom I recall spending hours working on large and difficult picture puzzles. "Lend me your eyes, Walter," she'd say, after a hearty lunch. "I can't find this piece."

Mother prepared me to approach Grandfather by telling me that I was named for my Uncle Walter, his eldest child, who died in a freak auto accident shortly after graduation from college. I can't say that I fully understood it at the time, but she said Grandpa was so grief stricken by the loss of Walter that he found little consolation in my father, his remaining son, whose qualities, he felt, simply couldn't compare with those of the boy he had lost.

"Imagine how hard that must have been for your father, Walter, always being compared with a dead hero!" she said. Perhaps that was why my father was so wrapped up in his work. Apparently Grandpa remained inconsolable, for when it came time for me to be born, Mother told me how Grandpa had stood under her bedroom window, pounding his cane on the brick terrace and crying out: "Is it a boy? Is it a boy? *Just tell me it's a boy!*"

When my parents returned from their trip, I took it upon myself to knock on Grandpa's door. I was surprised by his friendliness. I went back regularly, and his first question was always "Would you like to shoot?" to which I always answered yes, because I realized how it pleased him to teach me.

Unfortunately, I wasn't born to be an archer, as Grandpa would remind me by standing far back and planting his shaft well inside mine on the rare occasion when I came anywhere near the bull's eye. Often I thought how our contests must have stirred sad memories of much keener competition with his long lost son. But Grandpa appeared to enjoy the companionship as much as I did, and I began to realize that just possibly, my own father might be more approachable than I thought.

CHAPTER THREE

Arrival

Whenever Dad came to breakfast in his wool knickers, it usually meant he was planning a drive in the country. Sometimes he took me along, so I was disappointed when he said, "Not today, Walter, I have something special I need to do."

Something special? Perhaps something to do with my coming birthday – but what?

It was mid-afternoon when Dad returned with a large, sturdy wooden box under his arm. I noticed it had a pair of rope handles and some holes bored in the sides. Also, I thought I could hear scuffling sounds inside.

"So, you have it," Mother said, looking pleased.

"Sure do," said Dad with a grin. "Now Walter, we know your birthday isn't 'til next week, but what's inside this box is for you. We hope you'll like it and learn to take good care of it."

Whatever "it" was! Various creatures flashed through my mind: A puppy? Another rabbit? A guinea pig? Possibly a snake, or a turtle? (I *really* liked turtles!)

I was about to open the box when Dad exclaimed, "Hold on! On second thought, we'd best take that box down to the farm – no telling what might happen if we open it here," he said, with a wink at my mother.

At the farm, Dad set the box down carefully and went to haul a spare rabbit hutch out of the barn. "Here," he said, "Put the box inside this pen before you open it." I did, and then, cautiously, I raised the top. What a surprise! There, blinking in the bright sun, was the neatest, roundest, pink and tan creature you could imagine: an honest-to-goodness real live PIG!

We weren't prepared for what happened next. With a sudden flurry of short legs, the little creature upset the box and raced about the hutch's small runway, frantically trying to escape. "Close that screen" Dad shouted, "or we'll be chasing that animal 'til dark!"

Down came the top screen with a bang. Suddenly the little pig stood stock still.

Only its tail continued to squiggle. It looked up at us as if to ask, *Okay, so what's next?* "Remember," Dad warned. "Pigs are not like dogs, Walter. It may take some time before this one learns to trust you."

Excited, I knelt down to inspect my surprise. A small, wet snout snuffled my cheek as I pressed my face against the wire netting. Dad brought a bowl of water and gingerly I raised the screen just enough to put it in. The pig gulped it thirstily.

"A small, wet snout snuffled my cheek..."

"So what do small pigs eat?" I wondered aloud, "it must be hungry." When Dad didn't answer, I realized he'd gone to the hen house, leaving me alone to get acquainted with my small new friend.

"Well," Mother asked at supper. "So what do you think of your birthday present?"

"He's wonderful," I answered, with a grin. "But I never thought pigs were so fast!" Dad chuckled. "You'll just have to be faster, won't you? And you're right: It is a *HE*."

I was delighted, but I was also worried about Greenhorn. How would he take to this new creature in his yard, especially if my pig happened to get loose? *Even if he did*, I reassured myself, *there was no way that stupid goat could catch him!*

Next day I was up at the crack of dawn and down at the farm before breakfast. But my pig was nowhere to be seen, not in his runway or inside the hutch, or around the yard – it was a bad moment!

Then I heard a gentle wheezing. Lifting the wooden lid, I saw the tip of a pink snout peeking from the straw; hidden beneath it, my pig was sound asleep and snoring. I put the bowl of bread and milk close by in the runway. First, his snout began to twitch. Then he was on his haunches, shaking off the blanket of straw and blinking in the rising sun.

What a perfect creature! I thought, seeing things I had

missed in the previous day's excitement. Fine blond hairs, shading into tan over the shoulder, covered his body. The tops of his ears flopped forward, so that when his head was down you couldn't see his expression. The pink, rat-like tail never stopped twitching. As for the tiny cloven feet, they looked as if they were made of pink porcelain. *What a wonderful pig,* I said aloud, *What a special pig! And, best of all, I'm the only kid who has one!*

Did pigs like dry cereal? I hoped so, because every time the cereal companies came out with new ones, I sent away for samples. The cost was only a three-cent stamp. I'd been sending away for over a year; by now I had quite a collection. Samples that failed our breakfast test made perfect freight for the box cars of my electric train.

What about breakfast for a pig? They say pigs are picky eaters; he might not like some cereals any more than I did. But, if I mixed them together, perhaps he wouldn't know the difference; I'd just have to try it and see.

According to Dad, who got it from farmer Pritchard, who raised him, my pig was almost 2 years old. "You see, Walter," my father said, "your pig is special. He's a runt. That means he will always be the size he is now, no matter how old he gets to be. Mr. Pritchard told me he came from a litter of six; his five brothers and sisters are already more than twice as big."

I liked that idea. Perhaps I'd get to keep him longer than some other pets we'd had. Reading my thoughts, Mother said, "Yes, dear, he's yours as long as you feed him and look after him."

After breakfast, I carried a blue enamel dish with a mixture of reject cereals mixed with milk, carefully down the hill, trying not to spill any. My pockets were stuffed with greens for my rabbit and a big bunch of carrot tops to keep Greenhorn busy while I did my chores. My pig gave the mixture a few cautious sniffs. Then it was down to business, and the bowl was soon empty. Obviously, I wouldn't have to worry about his taste in cereal!

My tenth birthday also brought an assortment of books and toys. Nice as they were, they couldn't compare with my lively pig. In the evening, as I lay on the living room floor, looking at pictures of pigs in the encyclopedia, Mother said, "You know, dear, you've had that animal for a week now – don't you think it's time to give him a name?"

"I know, and I've been thinking – but I can't come up with one." Together we tried to think of a name, something more original than Snuffles, Porky, or Piglet. Finally Dad said, "Why not call him Cousin John?"

We didn't have a relative by that name, and even if we had, most people wouldn't think it complimentary to have a pig for a namesake. Dad's suggestion came from the story of a mischievous boy he recalled from his own childhood. This storybook "Cousin John" was curious, high-spirited, and often on the verge of trouble.

"I like it," said Mother. "Me, too," I said. So Cousin John he became.

CHAPTER FOUR

Doubting Thomas

You can't walk a pig without a harness. Because a pig's neck is as big around as its head, there's nothing to keep a collar from slipping off. So Dad and I went to see Homer Grimes at the Dog Emporium where a gold-on-black sign in the window proclaimed EVERYTHING FOR YOUR DOG – SHOW GROOMING A SPECIALTY.

Homer Grimes and his wife, Stella, raised purebred Pomeranians, small fluffy creatures that Mother said reminded her of powder puffs. Dad was less kind. He called them "toys for rich ladies with nothing better to do. If you want a real dog," he advised, "get a St. Bernard."

Mr. Grimes was tall and skinny. He wore steel-rimmed spectacles, a bow tie, and what appeared to be, regardless of the season, the same dark-gray suit and vest. (Of course, it was possible that he owned several suits of the same cut and color.)

Mr. Grimes also wore a vaguely worried expression, as if expecting that customers might have something to complain about. Dad had known the Grimes for many years. Homer

Grimes' somber manner always reminded him of an undertaker. "All he needs," Dad said, "is a pair of those sleazy gray gloves." Stella Grimes was just the opposite: short, stout, and cheerful. But we seldom saw her because she was mostly out back, grooming dogs.

Homer Grimes knew every dog worth knowing in our neighborhood, with or without its owner. Dogs were his life as well as his livelihood. Even a brief conversation would prompt him to point out two faded photographs taped to the side of the cash register: "Grand Duchess Marie" and "Princess Bira," two prize Poms that had won "Best in Class" at the Westminster Kennel Club show many years before.

Dad came right to the point. "Mr. Grimes, we need some sort of harness for an animal of about this size," he said, spreading his hands about two feet apart. "Aha" said Mr. Grimes confidently. "You must be wanting something for a cocker spaniel or possibly a young bulldog. I do believe we have just the thing for one of those fine breeds right over here."

He pointed to an elegant black leather harness with shiny brass studs hanging with many others from a row of pegs attached to the wall. Dad looked doubtful as Mr. Grimes reached for the harness and held it up for our inspection. "I am correct, am I not, that what you require is for a dog of the size I mentioned?"

"What we're looking for, Mr. Grimes, is not for a dog at all. What we need, in fact, is something we can use to walk a pig."

Homer Grimes made a sort of clucking sound, fumbled with his bow tie, removed his glasses, and, looking hard at my dad, asked softly, "Did you say pig?"

"Yes, PIG," Dad repeated with a trace of irritation, "A smallish pig. A runt pig, to be precise."

"A pig," murmured Mr. Grimes incredulously. "A small pig," he repeated, replacing his spectacles and looking anxiously about the shop in hopes of finding something to satisfy such an extraordinary request. "Ah yes, what about one of these?" he asked, pointing to a none-too-strong looking harness in rough brown leather. "We do have calls for them, now and again – for field work, don't you know," he added, with a hopeful look.

"No, Mr. Grimes, I'm afraid that won't do," Dad said firmly. "We'll take that well-made one you showed us with the brass studs, but in red leather, if you please."

Mr. Grimes nodded silently, looking more pained than usual, while Dad and I looked at each other, trying hard not to laugh. Red leather with brass studs! I grinned at the thought of how grand we'd look – Cousin John is his flashy harness and me in my new white Keds, parading down Heath Street together.

Dad paid for the harness and handed it to me. "Now, we'll

see," he said, and we left Mr. Grimes standing limply in the doorway, slowly shaking his head.

"You better try that harness on him inside the fence," Dad warned, "Chances are he won't like it, and you'll have your hands full. Remember, no matter what, don't let him loose!"

That afternoon, my cousin Tommy came to visit me from across the hill. "I hear you have a pig. Is he down at the farm? If so, I'd like to see him."

"Sure," I said, "let's go down. You can help me get him used to his harness. Dad thinks he may not like it at first, so we could have some problems."

I liked Tommy, even though we argued a lot. He was older than I was and, according to Dad, a better student, (which wasn't saying much!). How Dad knew that I never could figure out, because we went to different schools. Anyway, my cousin Tommy was okay because, unlike some other guys I knew, he always said what he thought, even if it was mostly negative.

Dad was right. Cousin John got squirmy the moment we tried to get the harness under his belly. He rolled back and forth on his back, working his stumpy legs as if he was running upside down. His small feet were sharp and several times he almost squirted away from us. I was really glad for Tommy's help.

Finally, after several close calls, we managed to secure the harness. Handing Tommy the leash, I picked up my pig and set him on his feet. To our surprise he just stood there, looking up at us, as if waiting to see what we expected of him next.

Tommy and I took turns walking Cousin John inside the fence. Greenhorn lowered his horns and pawed the ground each time we passed him – hardly the time for formal introductions!

More like a dog than I thought, I said to myself as Cousin John snuffled everything, pausing here and there to root into whatever took his fancy. A hard pull was needed to get him going again, in which I felt both his strength and his stubbornness.

I wanted to walk him up the hill and show him off to my family, but Tommy talked me out of it. "I think he's had enough for the first day," he said. So we returned Cousin John to his pen with a big dish of milk and apple cores, his favorite treat. Watching my pig scarf them up, Tommy said, "You know, my parents can't understand why you would want a pig for a pet. They say pigs are such dirty animals."

"Then they don't know much about them," I answered defensively.

"What do you mean?"

"Well, for a start, pigs have a problem: they don't sweat and they can't pant the way dogs do. It doesn't help them to stay cool to have their only sweat glands in their nose. That's why they like to wallow in mud in warm weather – it helps to cool them down."

"Really?" said Tommy doubtfully. "So what about the way they root around in garbage? Most people think that's a pretty filthy habit."

"Yeah, I know what most people think. But rooting is the way pigs hunt for food. If you watch them closely, you'll see they're very choosy about what they actually eat. A pig's nose is very sensitive – it tells him what's good to eat and what isn't. They can also close their nostrils to protect them from getting plugged up. Did you know that pigs learn to avoid poisons after just one try while horses never do?"

"Never heard that," replied Tommy, "So, okay, but what about their you-know-whats?"

"Look over there" I said, pointing to a neat pile in the far corner of the runway. "My pig may be a sloppy eater, but he always does his duties right there in the corner, never in or near his house."

"So you're saying most people are wrong about pigs," said Tommy with a grin suggesting he liked the idea.

"That's right. Pigs are actually clean animals, given half a chance. It's the way people keep them that makes them seem dirty. They're also very smart. Did you know that they can climb ladders?"

"Climb ladders? You've got to be kidding. How can a pig do that with such short legs and hard feet? Can your pig do that? If so, I'd sure like to see it!"

"As a matter of fact, he can't. Only piglets can."

"Thought so," said Tommy. "But Cousin John's a piglet, isn't' he? – so you're just putting me on."

"NO, I'm not," I said. "You see, Cousin John isn't a piglet at all. He's a runt. That's a small adult, a mini-pig, that won't grow any bigger. For some odd reason, only true piglets can climb."

"How do you know that?" Tommy asked, again looking dubious.

"Because I saw one do it at the circus. It went up one side of those folding ladders painters use, and down the other. Later I found out that people who train them need a supply of young piglets because they quickly grow too heavy to climb."

"Amazing," said Tommy, in a tone that suggested he still wasn't entirely convinced.

"Believe it or not, as you wish," I replied, irritated, as I often was by Tommy's doubts. "But one thing I know for sure: This pig's too hot, and that's not good. Since he doesn't have a wallow, we've got to find some way to cool him down. I have an idea that might work. If you help me take him out, and hold onto him, we'll try it."

"Cousin John stood stock still...
letting the cool water flow over him."

While Tommy held my pig, I screwed a nozzle onto a garden hose and slowly began to bathe him. Cousin John stood stock still, chin up, eyes closed, letting the cool water flow over him. His tail, a sure sign of his mood, had a tight, approving curl.

"Amazing," Tommy said again, this time with something like enthusiasm. "He actually *likes* being washed."

I wished I were a fly on the wall in Tommy's house that night, to hear him tell his parents what clean, clever, self-respecting creatures pigs really were!

CHAPTER FIVE

A Close Shave

As usual, Sunday lunch with assorted aunts and uncles was long and boring. Dad thought so, too, and I could tell by the nervous way he kept tugging at his collar. I was so impatient to get my pig harnessed for his first real outing that I passed up seconds on my favorite dessert, vanilla ice cream with hot butterscotch sauce.

Finally, after more family chit-chat over after dinner coffee, Dad managed to excuse us by saying "Walter needs me to help him walk his pig." While everyone looked at Mother for an explanation, I said "I'll get your heavy walking stick from the back hall, Dad, in case we meet up with any troublesome dogs."

Dogs were still allowed to run free where we lived, mostly the kind that Mr. Grimes would describe as "fine, well-bred animals."

When we reached Heath Street, several ladies in an open touring car stopped to let us cross over to the boardwalk on the other side. "What breed is that?" they teased, pointing and giggling. Ignoring them, Cousin John strained forward, tugging me after him. Again, I was surprised by his strength, considering the shortness of his legs.

The boardwalk echoed with the clip-clop of Cousin John's hard hooves as he pranced along, head high, harness gleaming, obviously pleased with himself. Now and then he pulled to the side to root in the grass. I had to yank hard on the leash to get him moving. We were headed for Dane's farm, where I knew Cousin John would find others of his kind, even if they would be many times his size.

During one of his rootings, I happened to look behind us: "Uh-oh, Dad," I exclaimed, "There's a bunch of dogs back there, and they're coming up fast!"

"Consarn it!" said Dad, "Just keep that animal moving!"

More dogs kept appearing from the yards we passed, intrigued by the scent my pig was leaving behind him. Soon we were surrounded by a yipping, snarling mob of canines, each of them eager for a good sniff at Cousin John's rear end. There were boxers and bulldogs, retrievers and setters, spaniels and poodles, a German Shepherd, and a big furry chow with an amazing purple tongue.

"I don't like this at all", Dad growled, swinging his stick to keep dogs clear of my bare legs.

No sooner did one dog shoulder up to the head of the line than another shoved it aside. Whenever one happened to touch Cousin John, he let out a high-pitched squeal and sprinted forward, towing me after him.

"Whatever happens, *keep hold of that pig!*" Dad yelled, landing some well-aimed blows on the larger, more aggressive dogs.

The jumble of scrambling legs, flailing tails, and snapping jaws threatened to trip me up. But thanks to Dad's stick and the momentum of my speeding pig, I managed to keep my feet.

Just then I realized that Cousin John had a secret weapon. Each time the leading dog closed in for what it expected would be a satisfying sniff, my pig revolved his rat-like tail in its face just like a miniature pink propeller!

This upset the lead dogs so much that they dropped out to fight with each other, until they noticed that the parade was leaving them behind. Then they'd race to catch up, only to be frustrated again. I was proud of my pig's clever defense, but worried that he might lose his tail!

Dogs continued to surge at my heels and mill about my bare legs. I wished I had the corduroy knickers and wool stockings I wore for school!

The pack grew meaner as we approached Dane's farm gate. Cousin John went faster still, and it was all I could do to hang on. Turning to defend our rear. Dad shouted, "Get through that gate as quick as you can – I'll try to keep this *!@*!@ gang outside!"

"Whatever happens, keep hold of that pig!"

I was just about to open the gate when a different dog suddenly appeared, a powerful, bad-tempered Doberman that everyone knew, and nobody liked. Neither did the other dogs. Turning on him as one, snapping and snarling, they ran him back where he came from.

"So much for Mr. Grimes and his pedigreed pals," Dad muttered grimly as we slipped through the gate and led an exhausted Cousin John to meet his portly relatives. The little pig looked up, and the great ones looked down, lowering their snouts and snorting their greetings through the bars. Cousin John responded with high, excited oinks. Was he telling them about our scary adventure? I wished I knew!

Just then I noticed a tear in Dad's knickers; it was a miracle we'd escaped being bitten!

Later, when describing our close shave to friends, Dad always made a special point of adding, "And there wasn't a St. Bernard in the bunch."

His admiration for St. Bernards began with a puppy he got when I was born. Dad named him Count of Porlock, and he quickly outgrew his first kennel, one of Mother's hatboxes with a hole cut in the side. He grew to be enormous, even for a St. Bernard. Growing up together, Porlock and I became fast friends. Almost from birth, Porlock became jealously protective of anyone belonging to our family. A growl from him was enough to keep dogs and strangers at a distance.

Even so, he was a gentle giant.

I was playing outside one day when several pheasant chicks happened to stray onto the lawn. Gently, silently, the huge dog picked them up in his slobbery jaws and one by one, returned them to safety in the long grass. Who could forget that?

Dad taught him to carry second class mail home from the post office, a trip of several miles across busy streets. The mail was sometimes soggy on arrival, but postman Porlock never lost a piece.

Shortly before Cousin John's arrival, my parents decided that Porlock would have to go. His intimidating size and protective disposition had become too much for visitors. They gave him to Mr. Walsh, our postman, who was retiring to New Hampshire.

It was a sad day for all of us, especially for me, because I wasn't allowed to give Porlock a parting hug or even watch him leave. Instead, I was told to sit on a small, green chair in the pantry and drink my orange juice. Such silliness only made things worse. I've disliked small green chairs ever since.

"Better take the back way home," Dad said, closing the Dane's farm gate behind us. "That's quite enough of dogs for one day." Cousin John looked so tuckered out that I scooped him up and carried him across the street to a path we hoped would avoid his tormentors.

Back at the house, Mother said, "I heard all that ruckus down there." Then, eyeing my bare legs and the tear in Dad's knickers, she asked, apprehensively. "Are you both okay?"

"Let's just say we survived," Dad said with a grin, "That little pig is something, plucky as well as fast. If you could have seen the way the dogs went for him! We had all we could do..."

"Good thing we brought the stick," I broke in. "It could have been a whole lot worse."

"And how is Cousin John, dear?"

"Really, really tired," I said. "But not even a scratch, as far as I can see. He's one lucky pig." And I told her how he used his tail.

After a full account of our adventures, Mother said, "I do hope you won't ever try that again," adding, with a sigh of relief, "And now let's have some tea."

Dad's praise for Cousin John's performance made me hopeful he would say something about mine. Instead, examining the tear in his knickers, he said, "I guess we proved we can walk a pig. Right, Walter?" I nodded, and he flashed one of his brief, enigmatic smiles.

CHAPTER SIX
Tales Out of School

On warm spring afternoons, I liked to stretch out on the grass beside Cousin John and tell him stories. It was fun to pretend he understood, even though I knew he didn't. Anyway, he was a good listener, and sometimes when I paused he'd roll his eyes as if to say, *Well, go on, go on.*

Because I couldn't take my pig to school, I told him all about what happened there – things I wouldn't tell anyone else, including my mother.

One day I described how we played marbles on our knees in the mud during recess, and how upset I was when I suspected my classmate Jimmie of taking one of my three prize agates from a leather pokey I left behind while I went to the bathroom.

"Aggies," I explained to Cousin John, "aren't your ordinary glass marbles. They're special because they're made of quartz, a natural rock that comes in different colors. Clever players are always trying to win more aggies by beating less clever ones, like me."

"I liked to stretch out...beside Cousin John and tell him stories."

"When I returned to the game," I continued, "there were only two of the three large agates I was sure were in my bag before I left. "Okay," I said, "so who's been fooling with my marbles?"

My friends Harry and Randy eyed each other, then both looked hard at Jimmie, a big fat slug of a boy who also happened to be our class bully. Avoiding their eyes, Jimmie studied his outsized sneakers. It was even more suspicious that he refused to empty his bag like the rest of us.

Words flew. Soon Jimmie, and I were scuffling in the mud. I tried to grab his bag while Harry and Randy looked on, and giggled. (I imitated the gurgling sound I made when Jimmie's big belly scrunched my face in the mud. At this, Cousin John pricked up his ears, appearing to be listening intently.)

Suddenly a pair of strong hands separated us and jerked us to our feet, "What's going on here?" demanded Mr. Anders, the football coach, a muddy boy in each fist. "He took *my* agate," I blurted out accusingly. "*Did NOT!*" Jimmie retorted. Coach Anders made each of us empty our pokey bags and pockets. Jimmie had three agates right enough, but to my surprise and embarrassment, my blue and white treasure was not among them.

"Must have swallowed it," said Harry sarcastically. "Yeah, wouldn't put it past him," said Randy, suggestively rolling his eyes. "Okay, you guys, that's enough," Coach Anders snapped.

None of us had ever seen Coach so angry. Our punishment? Six hours raking leaves after school, plus a report to each of our parents. Jimmie's time was for fighting, mine for making a false accusation. Coach said to the other two, "Since when do you sit on your hands while a big kid beats up on a smaller one? Is that your idea of sportsmanship? You'll get the same punishment as the others."

More heck awaited me at home, especially for messing up a nearly new pair of knickers. Was my four-legged listener sympathetic? He seemed to be, but again I couldn't really tell.

So what did happen to my prize agate? Answer: Nothing. To my shame, next morning I found it under my bed.

The worst punishment came on Monday when I had to apologize to Jimmie face to face. As I told my pig, "Just because someone looks guilty doesn't mean he is, and be careful if that someone is bigger than you!"

Few of the tales I told Cousin John were as lively as this one. I'm sure most were pretty boring to a smart pig, which was probably why he so often fell asleep.

CHAPTER SEVEN

Out in the Cold

A muffled thud, followed by another, echoed through the house, waking me up. *Must be Tom O'Sullivan, the ice man*, I said to myself, *making a delivery*. You could set your clock by Tom. Every Tuesday, at 6:30am, he parked his truck at the back door, and leapt out to check out our ice supply by squinting down the chutes leading to the cold boxes in the pantry below.

Then, if needed, he would hook his tongs into a hefty block of ice, sling it over his shoulder, back up to the chute, and let it go with a resounding crash. With many deliveries to make, Tom was usually in a hurry. But if he needed to rearrange his blocks, he'd stop long enough for me to ask him about his latest mix-up with dogs or some other misadventure.

Dogs were the bane of Tom's existence. Some just couldn't get used to his visits. They'd bark from the moment they heard his truck in the driveway until he left, rousing the entire household. It was good we no longer had a dog.

One morning I noticed Tom was limping. When I asked him about it he told me that the Osborne's big Doberman, the dog that nobody liked, went for him, causing him to slip and fall with a fifty-pound block on his back. "It's a bloody wonder I warn't killed," he said in his amiable brogue.

"So why do you keep going there?"

"It's me job," he answered simply. "You takes the rough with the smooth in my line o' work."

"I suppose you have to," I said, trying to be sympathetic. "But everyone knows that dog is a bully. They could at least tie him up."

"Just you try tellin' that to the likes o' them people," Tom said with a good-natured chuckle. Then, stroking his stubbly chin thoughtfully, he added, "But maybe they'd take it, comin' from the likes of you."

The Osbornes were the wealthiest family in our neighborhood. True, we didn't really *know* them. But people *said* that they had everything, including an indoor squash court, a bowling alley, and a swimming pool. Dad said they even had a full-size pipe organ in the parlor!

As I watched Tom limping with his load, I thought what a good thing it would be if *sometime* the Osbornes had to do without – like without ice, for example!

"To tell you true now," Tom continued, "there's only a few dogs like 'im in all the ones I see drivin' around. Sure an' there's some that'll carry on terrible whenever they sees me – must be the black apron and them tongs in me hand – but they don't go for me like he done."

Tom did look a bit scary. He was big and brawny, with huge hairy forearms, a face like a squashed potato, and several missing teeth. But as Dad often said, "There wasn't a kindlier man around." Just how kind he was, I was about to find out.

One blustery Monday night in March we had a heavy wet dump of snow. Next morning Tom had to wait at the bottom of the hill for "Dapper Dan" Callahan and his team of horses to plow the driveway.

Dan's nickname came from the way he rode the plow, sitting bolt upright in a neat tweed jacket, his fine features and wavy hair topped by a jaunty green cap. With a bearskin robe covering his knees, he looked like a king on a throne. A long, mean-looking whip stood in a holder beside him.

I loved to watch his team of Belgians work the plow. They were a rich chestnut color, with lighter manes and tails. Balls of snow beaded the hair around their massive hooves, making them appear even larger. Both horses wore leather blinders bearing the initials "DC" in brass, and a double string of bells across their chests jangled merrily as they moved. When they came after sundown, I was fascinated by the showers of sparks thrown up by the plow's iron shoe as it scraped along the driveway.

Several times I tried to approach the team with lumps of sugar, but Callahan would wave me away with a stern, "Stand clear there, Sonny," as he guided the team with a tug on the reins or a whistle.

One very early morning that winter, Tom and I were waiting for the circle to be cleared so he could head the ice truck downhill. Dan was having trouble getting around the big snow pile in the middle. Suddenly, snatching the long whip from its holder, he laid it on hard, again and again, across the horses' hind quarters. The terrible sound brought tears to my eyes, and I tried to shut it out by hiding behind Tom's rubber apron.

"There's no damn need for that," cried Tom. "Can't he see them creatures is doin' the best they can?" Then, looking down at me he said, "It ain't the first time I seen him do it – he's a cruel man who don't deserve them fine animals. Horses has feelin's. One o' these fine days, when he ain't expectin' it, they'll go for Dan Callahan in their stall." I never knew if anything happened to Dapper Dan, because I had lost all interest in him and his team.

But something else happened after I left Tom and went back in the house. As he told me later, "So there I was, sittin' in me truck, wonderin' how late I'd be with the rest o' me drops, when somethin' in the field caught me eye. *Hello*, I said, *that's a creature out there an' he's a way in over his head.*"

"So I scooped 'im up and set 'im on the seat beside me."

"So I hopped out to see what it was. *Mother o' Mary*, I said, *if it ain't the young feller's pig, an' he's near done up with strugglin'.* So I scooped 'im up and set 'im on the seat beside me. Perishin' cold he was, too, the poor little sod."

"So, when Callahan was done," Tom continued, "I took yer pig to the back door. *Kitchen's the place fer you, me lad,* I said, and I went in real quiet-like, an' set 'im down on one o' them flour sacks near the stove, where Cook can't miss 'im. Then I dropped off the ice."

That woke Nellie, the cook, as Tom knew it would. So the second thing I heard that frosty morning was a loud shout up the back stairs. "Come down then, Walter Paine, and get this bloomin' pig out o' me kitchen."

With no idea how Cousin John got there in the first place, I was both amazed and alarmed. Racing down the kitchen stairway two steps at a time, I found Nellie tugging on something half under the stove. "I gave him some slops earlier," she said in a kindly tone, "and now the divil himself wouldn't raise him."

A healthy pig's tail is tightly curled. Cousin John's hung limp and straight, hardly a good sign. "Sure and it was a lucky thing for the both of you that Tom's the kind of man he is," said Nellie, as she hustled us toward the back door. "Thanks, Nellie," I said, snuggling Cousin John under my jacket, "It sure is."

All the way to the barn I asked myself how could my pig possibly have gotten out, with the stall bolted and the barn doors tight shut?

Despite his close call, it turned out that Cousin John was none the worse for wear. But his escape remained a mystery, until spring, when I went to clean his stall.

In the far right corner, under a wad of straw, I found a big hole, possibly made by rats trying to raid Cousin's John's food. My pig must have tumbled through it, into the cold, dark crawl space under the barn. Scared and unable to get back to his cozy straw bed, he probably panicked and ran out into the storm.

The rescue confirmed what Dad said about Tom. But for him, I would have lost my precious pig! I thought that a letter to the Osbornes about their dog might be a good way to thank him. But before I could send it, we heard that their wretched Doberman had been run over by a coal truck. As Tom said, with a toothy grin, "Sometimes it's the Good Lord takes care o' them things."

CHAPTER EIGHT

In and out of a Jam

After his summer in a larger yard, Cousin John was unhappy with his smaller quarters at our farm. Because he also needed a snug place for winter, we decided to convert a former pony stall in the barn for his use. On warmer days, he could still go outside where there was space to root and snooze in the sun. I liked the new arrangement because I could feed him inside the barn without fear of Greenhorn butting in.

One night there was an unfortunate accident. While we were away at the shore, a skunk decided to move in under the barn. You could tell one was around by the triangular pockets it made in the grass while searching for insects.

Then there was that smell – unmistakable from the house and overpowering at the barn itself. Skunks are timid creatures, and perhaps it was frightened by my pig during the night. But poor Cousin John! His eyes were so swollen he could barely see. It hurt me to watch him try to relieve the pain by rubbing his sensitive snout in the dirt.

I did my best to comfort him with the hose and a heavy lather of soap. But it didn't work. *Why wasn't it you, you stupid goat,* I growled at Greenhorn who watched us intently. Cousin John's suffering had me very upset. How I wished Dad would get home, so I could ask him what to do! When he finally did, the stink rising from the farm was enough to tell him what had happened.

"You might try plastering him with raw tomatoes," Dad suggested. "Once we had a spaniel that tangled with a skunk. Raw tomato helped, as I remember. Why don't you take a few spoiled ones and rub them all over him."

Raw tomatoes!! Neither Cousin John nor I thought it funny, but we must have been a comical sight, slathered all over with white seeds and squishy red pulp. However, Dad's remedy did seem to help. Next day, Cousin John was almost his spunky self again.

The answer to my frequent question "Can I take my pig to school?" was always no. Instead, Mother suggested taking him to visit relatives. "Your pig lives so close to Aunt Grace and your Granna at the bottom of the hill – why not take him there?"

Next day, I was surprised by a call from Aunt Grace. "We've never met your famous pig," she said. "Why don't you bring him over for a visit?"

We had had a late fluke snowstorm that year, and Cousin John disliked snow – which you could tell by the narrow track in his runway, a straight line between the far corner where he did his duties and his inside retreat. The day happened to be warm and sunny. But with a foot or more of snow still on the ground, I decided to take him visiting in my green stake wagon. As a precaution, I put on his harness and leash.

Cousin John sat quietly on his haunches as I rang Granna's doorbell. My aunt opened the door. "So this is your famous pig," she said, eyeing him cautiously as if I might be planning to bring him in the house.

"Cousin John doesn't like snow," I explained, "but he'll be okay here in the wagon. Do you have something like celery or an apple he could eat?"

"Why yes, we do," said Aunt Grace, looking relieved. "Why don't you put him out front where your Granna can admire him, too?"

"Thanks, Auntie, I will," I said, and I began to haul the cart around to the living room window where Granna motioned me to come closer. I gave Cousin John an apple, but I forgot to hitch his leash to the wagon.

It happened that this aunt of mine spent much of the year in France. She spoke French like a native. She, too, had a close companion, a pampered wire-haired terrier named Jam, who spent each night on the foot of her bed. According to my aunt, Jam had been so well brought up that he answered only to those who spoke French.

I was about to leave Cousin John for a short visit inside with Granna when Jam came bounding around the corner of the house, barking furiously and heading straight for the wagon. Startled by the leaping, yapping dog, Cousin John vaulted clear of the cart and took off as fast as his short legs could carry him, trailing his leash through the snow.

At that moment my aunt appeared, galoshes flapping, "*Oh, mon dieu,* how stupid! I should never have let him out," she cried. "*Non, Jam, non! Mechant, mechant! Vien ici, cet instant.*" But Jam, who supposedly responded only to French, ignored her completely and lit out after my pig.

Snow flew as both animals tore about the yard. The noisy terrier gained on the straightaway only to lose ground when my speeding pig suddenly changed direction. I could see that Cousin John was tiring, and I was sick with worry about what would happen if the dog caught up with him when, suddenly, incredibly, he simply disappeared!

How could he have vanished in a yard completely enclosed by a high brick wall? There was only one possibility: a deep, stone-lined pit surrounding a large tree at the far end. Just then I noticed Granna waving vigorously in the same direction.

Fearing the worst, I ran to the pit, dropped to my knees and peered anxiously over the edge. There lay my small friend, eyes closed and motionless, half covered with snow! My heart stopped.

"Startled by the leaping, yapping dog,
Cousin John vaulted clear of the cart."

"He's dead; he must be!" I cried out. *And all because of my stupid carelessness!* It was a terrible moment.

Through my tears, I could see Aunt Grace coming toward me with a short ladder. Quickly I lowered it into the pit and scrambled down. Just as I bent over to touch him, Cousin John opened an eye and struggled feebly to get up. "He's alive, ALIVE!" I shouted, scooping him up and clambering back up the ladder.

"Oh, thank God for that," Aunt Grace exclaimed, with a sigh of relief. "Now we must get him to the vet, *tout de suite.* As for that wretched dog of mine, he'll hear from me later!"

Dr. Toby prodded Cousin John all over. He examined his joints, shone a light in his eyes, listened to his heart and chest. "You're really lucky, son," he said. "Your pig will be quite all right. What he needs now is food, water, and a nice long rest."

Boy, was I relieved! Just like his namesake in Dad's story, my friend was lucky. But the experience put an end to visiting in winter and any fondness I might otherwise have had for spoiled, twitchy terriers.

CHAPTER NINE

Beetle Hunters

I had many reasons to like the family friend we called "Dr. Tom," a naturalist at the Harvard Museum of Comparative Zoology in nearby Cambridge. But he was seldom there because he preferred to be off in the wilds, hunting for unusual reptiles.

Dr. Tom was one visitor I could count on to clamber up two flights of stairs to my growing "museum" in the attic. Sometimes he also brought me things collected on his travels, such as colorful tree snails from Cuba or spectacular insects from the jungle.

Although he came mainly to see my parents, I was especially fond of him because he always made time for me, either to teach me something about nature or to ask me serious questions, as if even a 10-year-old boy might have useful observations.

Mostly we talked about beetles because Dr. Tom knew how much they interested me. He liked to compare beetles with the knights of old I'd read about. Like them, he explained, beetles had a suit of armor to protect them in a world where softer creatures were often squashed or eaten. "Also, Walter," he said, "a beetle's armor helps to keep its insides from drying out, allowing these insects to live most anywhere, including the desert. And, because most beetles can fly, they can go wherever they like in search of food."

One night his questions had to do with numbers. "Any idea of how many different kinds of beetles there are, Walter? No? Well, take a guess."

"Maybe...a thousand?"

"Oh, many more than that," he said, smiling. "According to my scientific friends, America alone has at least 15,000 kinds, and more than 100,000 are known from the rest of the world. Just think what that means, Walter! It means that if you could put one of each living plant and animal in a row, one out of every five would be a beetle. That's why many scientists believe that beetles may be the most successful creatures alive."

"Amazing," said Dad, who had been listening intently.

"Yes," said Dr. Tom, "it certainly is, and there are thousands more just waiting to be discovered in those tropical jungles I like to explore."

Even my mother, who wasn't fond of "creepy-crawlies," liked to hear Dr. Tom describe his adventures. He was a big, heavy man who used his whole body to tell a story. He could be very funny, especially about himself. Once he got so carried away while telling how he chanced to find a rare reptile that he broke one of our antique dining room chairs.

One evening, as he was about to leave, he looked at me and said, "By the way, Walter, how's that splendid pig?" Mother gave me a quick look which said, *Not now, dear, not when he's trying to leave.*

"Fine," I answered, ignoring her. "We go on rambles together, and last week he helped me find something really good."

"He did? Well, tell me about it," said Dr. Tom, plunking down his briefcase.

"You know, Dr. Tom, how my pig likes to root? Well, that's okay most of the time. But it's a big bother when I'm hunting beetles because he always wants to snuffle just where I want to look and..."

"I imagine that's because he smells something," he interrupted. "Remember, a pig's nose is much more sensitive than ours. They can smell things as far away as twenty feet, even when they're buried underground. That's why the French use pigs to hunt for truffles, a special kind of edible fungus. But go on."

"Well, usually I have to tie him up so I can work. But this time I didn't. I let him root around while I turned over logs, looking for ground beetles. I wasn't having much luck, when suddenly I heard a loud squeal, and I saw my pig squirming around in a circle, dragging his nose in the dirt."

*"Suddenly I heard a loud squeal, and I saw
my pig squirming around in a circle."*

"I went to him and there was a big, shiny brown insect, on its back, working its legs in the air. I was excited because I knew what it was – a really BIG stag beetle, like the picture in my insect book! Nearby, I saw an old maple tree with a rotten hole at the bottom – my pig must have been rooting there when the stag clamped onto his nose."

"No wonder he squealed!" Dr. Tom exclaimed, "Those guys can really nip."

"If you can wait a minute I'll show him to you," I said, sprinting upstairs and down again with my prize, spread and mounted as Dr. Tom had taught me.

"Good work, Walter," he said. "That's a fine big male, not at all that common because they need so much time in the wood to become full grown. I suggest you search there again, and I'll bet you find more of 'em."

Dr. Tom smiled as he read the label: "Taken by my pig from a rotten maple tree. Brookline, Mass. May, 1933."

As he was leaving, Dr. Tom said, "You know, Walter, you and your helpful four-legged assistant should try poking about at night with a flashlight: You'll be surprised how many critters you'll find that you won't see during the day." As he shook his friend's hand, Dad said dryly, "I believe, Tom, that Walter already knows something about that."

CHAPTER TEN

Escape

For a second season we rented a house on the seashore north of Boston. It was cooler than Brookline and great fun to be close to a beach. Just as I liked to do at home, I was up at dawn and off to the shore to see what the night tide had brought in. An amazing number of different critters hid out in seaweed! I tried to decide whether they came from the land or the sea and made crude sketches of them in my notebook to look up later in the library.

Twice a week, Mr. Cronin, a part-time policeman, gave me swimming lessons. Curiously, I was much better under water than on top of it. There were also other boys my age to play with. We flew kites, built sand castles, and thought up pranks to play on unsuspecting grown-ups. We had a good one for dozing nannies, especially the grumpy ones who were always at us for kicking up sand near their precious infants.

Carefully, on hands and knees, we'd sneak up behind a dozing nanny's beach chair. Then we'd dig a hole, leaving just enough sand at the sides to support the frame. Finally we'd fill the hole with pails of water and stroll casually down the beach to await the result. It wasn't long in coming. If nanny made the slightest move, she was done for. If not, the water soon dissolved the sand and into the hole she went, white-stockinged legs in the air. Rescue from this undignified position required assistance, exposing her wet backside and increasing her mortification, to the great satisfaction of her young tormenters.

One morning I decided to take Cousin John for a walk on the beach. He didn't like it: too many dogs and the sand was too soft for his short legs. But he liked his summer quarters, which gave him more room than at home to root, snooze in the sun or watch what the rest of us were doing.

Our nearest neighbors were the Dennys. Mrs. Denny spent a lot of time in her garden. Dr. Denny, her husband, was a special friend of mine because he once brought me a pair of giant cockroaches he caught in the basement of the local hospital. He made me promise never to tell a soul where they came from, and I never did. The collection label read: "Taken inside a building, at Beverly, Mass."

One morning during breakfast the telephone rang. It was Mrs. Denny next door, and the look on Mother's face told me she had to be very upset. "Oh Charlotte, I'm *so* sorry," Mother said, "I'll send him over right away."

Frowning at me, Mother explained. "Mrs. Denny thinks

your pig got loose in her garden last night and rooted up many of her best plants. Now you get right over there, young man, and bring that pig back here. And don't forget to tell her how sorry you are!"

I sprang up, grabbed the harness and made a dash for the door as Mother called after me, "You must have left his pen open last night."

I was sure I hadn't, but never mind. All I cared about right then was that my precious pig was loose. Also, it was Friday. I dreaded not finding Cousin John before Dad arrived for a cool, quiet weekend after a scorching week in Boston. I found Mrs. Denny waving her arms at Michael, the Irish gardener we shared with several neighbors.

"He's made a pig's breakfast of it surely," said Michael, wringing his tweed cap between his hands and staring in disbelief at the jumble of plants and bulbs, some nibbled, some not. Then, seeing how upset I was, he laid a callused hand on my shoulder. "Come along then, young fella," he said, "an' we'll find 'im."

I tried to apologize to Mrs. Denny, but she waved me away. "First things first," she said. "You just go along with Michael – I'm sure he'll help you find your pig." We scoured the neighborhood, asking everyone we met if they'd seen a small pig. Sadly, no one had. *Try to think like a pig*, I told myself: *If you were Cousin John, where would you go?* "Don't worry, lad,"

Michael said reassuringly. "Chances are he ain't gone far, if I knows pigs."

Michael did know pigs. His stories about growing up in Ireland were full of them. To hear him tell it, you might have thought that pigs were more important than people. "The Irish have a saying," he said, "A pig is the gentleman that pays the rent."

My hopes had begun to fade as our search took us past the Denny's house for the second time. Just then we both heard a faint "oink." It appeared to come from somewhere under the house.

"There now, and what was I just tellin' you! *Himself* is in under there," said Michael, pointing to the foundation. "We can get 'im right enough, but we'll be needin' some help."

By now the entire neighborhood, including Tom Flaherty, the town's burly police chief, knew there was a pig on the loose. Young and old came to assist. Suppose you were Cousin John, squinting into the bright sunlight from the blackness under the house and all you could see was more than a dozen pairs of arms and legs coming closer and closer – Wouldn't you feel a sense of panic?

Michael, who knew pigs, had a plan. He told everyone, except me, to stand close around a small doorway in the lattice surrounding the foundation. Then, handing me a long bamboo pole, he said "Go around, you, to the back side and slide this pole through them laths, and when I give the sign, you start 'im." My pig, he predicted, would come out the door and into the many pairs of hands ready to catch him.

I could just make out Cousin John's outline in the gloom, as I slowly, carefully nudged the pole closer to his backside. Beyond the door I could see the tops of Michael's heavy boots.

"Start 'im then!" Michael cried, swinging the door open. For a moment nothing happened because the pole was a bit too short to reach my pig. Just then I lost my grip, and the pole clattered to the ground.

That did it! A pink and tan cannonball exploded out the door, clean through the thicket of hands, arms and legs, and disappeared, as far as anyone could tell, in the general direction of the beach.

"Streak o' light," Michael muttered ruefully, "Just a streak o' light. Sure an' there's naught so distractin' as a pig on the loose."

"*WOW*, is that pig ever fast, exclaimed my friend Larry, admiringly. "Sure is," I agreed sadly, worried sick that something bad was about to happen to my small friend.

Racing ahead to the stairway above the beach, I met a large woman in a bright yellow bathing suit splashed with purple flowers. She was dragging a beach chair and parasol behind her up the steps.

"Did you ever?" she wheezed, toiling slowly past me, "They

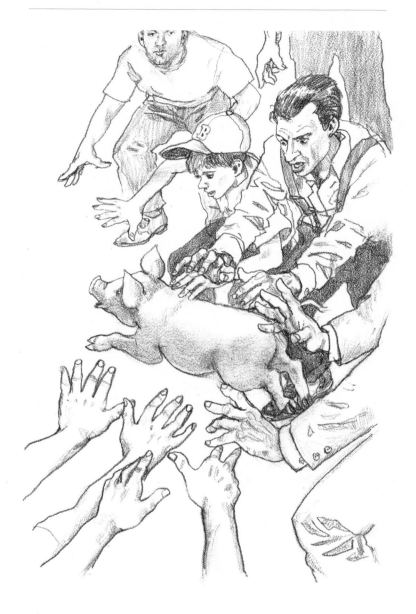

"A pink and tan cannonball exploded out the door."

say there's a pig on the beach. Would you believe that? *A Pig!*"

"Good! I'm glad," I said. "Where is he?"

"My, but you're a fresh young man, aren't you!" she said, eyeing me disapprovingly. Obviously, she didn't know about Cousin John.

Anxiously, I scanned the beach for some sign of him. Soon Michael joined me. "Look there," he said, pointing to a semicircle of bathers gathered around something small on the sand. "Sure, an' it must be 'im!"

My poor pig, I thought, *how tired and scared he must be, especially with so many people and dogs around!* "Can't we DO something?" I asked Michael imploringly.

"Sure an' we can; I'll just call down to Tom."

Chief Flaherty stood below us in his white cap, hands on hips, watching the crowd. "Halloo, Tom," Michael yelled, "You'd be doin' us a big favor if you'd just tell all them people to move back and pay less mind to that creature out there!"

The Chief must have been thinking the same thing, because he was already moving toward them, waving his arms and blowing his whistle. I could see Coach Cronin and lifeguard Punky Stone in her black rubber bathing cap, moving in the same direction.

We saw Cousin John clearly now, looking very small and forlorn, as he squatted on the sand with his back to the sea. Once again, Michael had a plan. "Now, sonny," he said. "you lick on home and ask Cook for the finest pail o' slops that ever a pig could want, and I promise you, we'll get 'im back."

I ran as fast as I could, returning with a big mess of potato peelings, apple cores, corn meal mush in milk, and the harness.

There were fewer people now, as we crossed the beach to where Cousin John lay stretched out on the cool wet sand with his forelegs tucked under him. "The poor little sod," Michael muttered sympathetically, "He's all tuckered out."

"He is, surely," echoed Chief Flaherty.

Once again, Michael was right. Cousin John wobbled to his feet and began to slurp the milk. Then he devoured the rest, beginning with the apple cores, his favorite. As I sat down beside him, he gave me a quick look that said, *it's all right now* and went on munching and snuffling until the bowl was clean. Then, with a whistling sound like air escaping from a beach ball, he settled on his side and closed his eyes.

He barely moved as I stroked his ears, slipped on the harness and scooped him up with tears of joy and relief. Trudging back across the squeaking sand, Michael held up the empty bowl and said with a toothy grin, "There's more than one way to catch a pig, includin' a streaker like 'im."

That evening, with my friend safely back in his pen, Mother sent me over to apologize properly to Mrs. Denny. Again, I was surprised by how nice she was to me, considering the damage to her precious garden.

I soon learned why. It seemed that a boy visiting a family across the road had noticed Cousin John in our yard. Early the following morning, he tried to play with him, and accidentally let him out. As Mrs. Denny explained what must have happened, I was thinking: *It's a good thing that kid has already gone back to wherever he came from!*

Dad chuckled at our account of the day's adventures. "I'd say you were very lucky," he said. "But let it be a warning. You might not be so lucky again." That night I went to bed tired but happy. Cousin John was safe and I knew for sure he trusted me and that we were truly friends.

CHAPTER ELEVEN

The Fair

Every summer neighboring towns held a fair. There were ox and horse pulls, riding contests, prizes for the best pets, the finest farm animals, the heaviest squash and watermelon, and the tastiest cakes and pies.

At the fairground's center, a brightly painted carousel revolved in time with tunes from a steam calliope. There were row upon row of stalls where, for a penny a toss, you could try to knock over and win stuffed animals, test your marksmanship on revolving metal targets, or throw darts at balloons.

There were people selling candied apples and pink cotton candy, but my favorite was the Good Humor man, ringing his bell and pedaling his cart full of candy-coated ice cream bars.

People came to the fair from miles around – it was the high point of the summer season. The more I read about it in *The Tattler,* our local weekly, the more I wanted to enter Cousin John, not as a pet, but in the farm animal division.

"I'll bet they've never seen a pig walking on a leash," I said to Mother, hoping she'd say, "Why don't you try it?" Instead she put me off, saying "Your father and I will have to talk about that."

A week before the fair I asked again. This time Mother said, "Perhaps dear, but you'd better talk to Daddy about it," adding "And if I were you, I think I'd wait 'til after dinner."

One of the best things about our summers by the sea was the opportunity to do more with my father. He had an old rowing scull from college days, which he had fitted with a seat so I could go along. I was timid at first because sculls are very tippy. But on calm days, with only the wake of passing motorboats to worry about, I soon came to enjoy skimming across the bay like one of the graceful terns that wheeled and dipped above us.

Some evenings Dad would read aloud from *The Black Arrow, Kidnapped, Treasure Island,* or *Robinson Crusoe,* the same classics he had enjoyed as a child. Dad's impersonation of the characters, plus the dramatic illustrations of N.C. Wyeth and others, made those stories come alive. Now and then, incidents in these tales would remind Dad of something from his own childhood, giving me an opportunity to learn a bit more about him.

Children can get weird ideas about their parents. One of mine was that the difficulties I was having with my father were somehow my fault. I had assumed that I had done something to irritate him, but I was now coming to understand that, often as not, the cause was a very busy or bad day at the office, or simply indigestion.

It was after one of Dad's readings that I screwed up the courage to ask him if I could enter my pig at the fair.

To my surprise, Dad said, "Yes, you may, but you must be extra careful. Your pig has never been where there's likely to be so much noise and confusion. He may not like it and try to get away." This was good advice, considering Cousin John's recent escapade.

My pig and I went into training. We practiced walking in harness every day. Deviations weren't allowed, except to pee. We even went downtown where, as usual, Cousin John attracted a lot of attention. Everywhere people stopped, stared, and said "Look at that, *a baby pig on a leash!*" I began to imagine what they'd say when we appeared at the fair!

One day, I borrowed Mother's ivory-framed mirror so Cousin John could see how splendid he looked in his red harness and shiny brass studs. But the pig in the mirror puzzled him. He "oinked" all over it, trying to identify the stranger's smell. Afterwards, Mother knew exactly where it had been.

"Does your pig go inside the house?" was a frequent question. I said, "No, but he could. Pigs are clean animals, you know." Their doubtful expression told me they didn't. After all, most people don't know much about pigs.

One day, a big, sour-looking man in a snap-brim cap said, "That pig of yours will soon be too big to walk." "No he won't," I replied. "He's a runt, you see; they don't get any bigger."

"Well then, sonny," said the man, with an evil grin, "That's unlucky for the both of you, isn't it?"

I didn't understand what he meant, and I surely didn't like the way he said it. Later I saw the man again, making deliveries from a blood-red panel truck with fancy gold decorations. On the side, under the picture of a boar's head, it said MEATS, WITH YOUR APPROVAL. I knew then that I was right to dislike him!

The day of the fair dawned hot and clear. I washed Cousin John under the garden hose with Dad's favorite, Packer's Pine Tar Soap. It came in a shiny metal box and smelled just like a sail-making loft. But I could never understand how *black* soap could make *white* lather! Anyway, Cousin John liked it, too, except when it got in his eyes. Finally, I polished his harness, and Mother made a rosette of red ribbons to fasten on top. My pig looked positively splendid!

To get Cousin John accustomed to the din at the fairgrounds, we decided to get there early and have a picnic lunch. Dad was right. It was a rowdy jumble of animals and people, so noisy that we couldn't understand much that came from the loudspeaker.

Horse pulls, ox pulls, and riding contests took up the long, hot morning. After lunch, animal judging was due to begin. We picnicked under a big oak tree at the edge of the fairgrounds, where Dad had his usual bottle of Bass Ale, and Cousin John snoozed on his green blanket, tethered to the foot of a heavy bench.

Animals and their owners were on the move from the long row of pens. Finally, the call I'd been waiting for came through the loudspeaker: "Ladies and gentlemen, your attention, please. We're about to judge the Swine Division. Owners and breeders will please assemble at the judges' tent."

I gave Cousin John a final touching up and walked him to the tent where the head judge, a burly, red-faced man with a broad smile said "I'm awful sorry, son, but we don't have a small class this year. Just look over there." Huge porkers, bigger than I'd ever seen, grunted and shuffled in their straw-filled pens, making the heavy timbers shudder as they lurched against them.

Seeing how unhappy I was, the judge said, "Tell you what, son. How would it be if we did something different with your pig?"

"Like what?" I asked defensively.

"Well, do you suppose you could walk your pig around that small pony ring over there?"

"You bet I can," I said quickly, relieved not to be turned away.

"Well then," said the judge, "you just bring him on when I announce it, after we judge that batch of hogs. Your pig's a male, isn't he?" he asked, stooping down for a closer look. "What's his name?"

"Cousin John" I replied, proudly.

"That's real fine, son – this will be something special. I doubt there's many folks here today who've seen a pig walking on a leash."

"How many times should I go around?" I asked.

"Oh, I should think once will do just fine, son. If the crowd really likes him, then I suppose you could go 'round again. Let's just wait and see."

Finally, after what seemed an eternity, an announcement came from the loudspeaker. "And now, ladies and gentlemen, if you'll just move across to the pony ring, we have something special for you: a young man with a runt pig that he has taught to walk on a leash. The pig's name, by the way, is "Cousin John." That drew a ripple of laughter from the crowd, which began to drift toward the pony ring where, at a signal from the judge, my pig and I were off at a fast clip.

Cousin John was at his best, snout high, picking up his feet and never once pulling to the side to root or snuffle. He seemed to like the crowd's attention. Once, twice we circled the ring, and were set to go round again when the judge

"There you are," said the judge...with a well done *to both of you!"*

signaled me to pull up. Children who missed the performance were shouting, *"Again, do it again!"*

"Son, that was just fine! He may be small but that's a real special animal you've got," said the judge, adding, "Just you stay right here – I'll be right back."

He disappeared into his tent, returning in a moment with something in his hand. "Now then," he said, bending down to pin a green ribbon with the words SPECIAL MENTION printed in gold, next to the red rosette on Cousin John's harness. "There you are," said the judge, straightening up, "with a *well done* to both of you!"

I didn't know what to do or say. Mumbling my thanks, I shook the judge's hand and made two quick bows in the general direction of the spectators who whistled and cheered. Then I hugged my friend so hard I made him squeal.

Mother said, "Cousin John's a born performer, dear – you should be very proud of him." I thought I heard Dad mumble something that sounded like "good work" into the hood of his big Graphlex as he snapped a picture of me on my knees, telling Cousin John just how great he was. In every way, it was a day to remember!

CHAPTER TWELVE

Reprieve

It was our last summer together, and Cousin John and I were inseparable. I even tried to take him punting. He didn't like it. His horny feet couldn't grip the boat's bottom, and he slid from side to side with each dip of my paddle.

We spent a lot of time downtown together, where Cousin John was happier now that all dogs had to be on a leash. I had learned to keep a sharp eye on him, especially after the disaster at Giulio's market where he snacked on everything within his reach, just as I was telling someone what a good pig he was!

Everywhere we went, people stopped and said, "Oh, so you're the boy with the little pig!" Most of my summer friends had pets. But none could compare with Cousin John when it came to getting attention.

It was September already, and I wished more than ever that summer would never end. I didn't like the idea of going home to get ready for boarding school. What was really bothering me was the thought of parting with my pig. I kept remembering what Mother said two years ago: "He's yours...*as long as you can take care of him*." The time would soon come when I couldn't.

Day and night I worried about what would happen to my small friend. Would he disappear like the pet lambs we bottle-fed one spring which came back as tiny chops and small fleece coats? Would he vanish suddenly, like our prize rooster, only to reappear as a Sunday roast? That's what often happened to animals on a farm, and the thought of it made me sick!

My parents noticed my hang-dog look and meager appetite. Recalling when he was first sent away to school, Dad was convinced my moping had to do with leaving home. "Don't worry," he said, "there'll be new friends and a lot going on – you'll soon get over it."

Mother knew what was really on my mind: Boarding school would be a temporary separation from home, but saying good-bye to Cousin John would be for keeps.

One day, while sewing name tapes on every stitch of my clothing, she called me over. "Here," she said, handing me a pair of socks, "Roll these up and put them in your trunk." Then, putting down her needle, she drew me close. "Something tells me that it's not going away to school but the thought of parting with your dear pig that's bothering you; am I right?"

"That's mostly it," I replied, head down, fighting tears. "I want so much to keep him...but I know I can't."

"You know, dear, there are times when we must part with someone or something we love very much. I know it's hard, but it's part of life that sooner or later each of us must learn to accept."

"I suppose so," I said forlornly, remembering Porlock's unhappy departure. More miserable by the minute, I blurted out, "So, what IS going to happen to Cousin John?"

Mother's answer was not what I expected. "Your father and I have been talking about that," she said. "He suggested that Dick Pritchard, the farmer who raised your pig, might be willing to take him back. Last night, Daddy called him up, and Mr. Pritchard said yes, he'd be happy to. The Pritchards have young children who would take good care of Cousin John. After all, he's a rather special pig, the way you've trained him."

Relief, mixed with pride, must have lit my face. Smiling, Mother said, "We suspected you'd like that. We also thought you might want to deliver him yourself, next weekend, after we get home."

"Oh, yes, I would," I said, giving her a big hug. In bed that night, the more I thought about taking my small friend back to his birthplace, the more I liked it, especially for him. The following Saturday, with Dad at the wheel and Cousin John and me in the rumble seat, we drove out to the Pritchard's farm where we found a boy about my age and his two younger sisters.

Wanting to surprise them, their father hadn't yet told them. They thought we'd come just for a visit. How their faces beamed when I said that Cousin John was back to stay!

Naturally I told them everything I'd learned: what he liked for treats, how to bathe him with a hose, how to put on his harness so it wouldn't slip. I also told them some of our adventures. I think they liked the one about Mrs. Denny's garden best.

Finally, it was time to give Cousin John a final hug, say my good-byes to the Pritchards, and get back in the car. I had been thinking that Dad was waiting for me, and we'd leave quickly. But we didn't. Dad was busy talking hens with Mr. Pritchard, comparing our Rhode Island Reds with his flock of Plymouth Rocks.

At last he got in beside me, and we drove slowly away. I didn't look back, trying hard to control my tears. For a time we drove in silence. Then, reaching over to lay his hand on mine. Dad said, "It's all right, Walter, I know how you've been worrying. The Pritchards are kind people. We can be sure that Cousin John has found a good home."

He said "WE!" Startled, I glanced up at him and saw what looked like a tear in the corner of his eye. More than words,

"It's all right, Walter...Cousin John has found a good home."

that said he understood and shared my fondness for the small creature we had just left behind.

Mother was right: Cousin John was no ordinary pet, and I would find it hard to be without him. But now, with Dad's understanding, it was going to be a whole lot easier.

Back home, Mother was surprised by my sudden cheerfulness. She must have wondered just what had brought it about!

I kept the ribbon from the fair, and Dad's photo, above the mirror on my bureau. They reminded me of what a special friend Cousin John had been, as happy with me, in his own proud, piggy way, as I had been with him. After all, it was mostly because of him that I became closer and more comfortable with my father, for which both of us would have so many reasons to be thankful over the years to come.

The care of Cousin John afforded me an invaluable lesson in responsibility, and the joy that came with it. The experience has stayed with me throughout my life. My hope for all young readers of this story is that you may be given a similar opportunity, and that your care and love may one day bring you the trust and companionship of a special creature like my Cousin John.